Muhammad صلى الله عليه وسلم
and
Islam

Kerena Marchant

Smart Apple Media

Great Religious Leaders

The Buddha and Buddhism   Jesus and Christianity
Guru Nanak and Sikhism   Muhammad ﷺ and Islam
Krishna and Hinduism   Moses and Judaism

First published by Hodder Wayland, 338 Euston Road, London NW1 3BH, United Kingdom
Hodder Wayland is an imprint of Hodder Children's Books, a division of Hodder Headline Limited.
This edition published under license from Hodder Children's Books.

Text copyright © 2002 White-Thomson Publishing Ltd
2/3 St. Andrew's Place, Lewes, E Sussex, BN7 1UP, UK

Edited by Margot Richardson, Designed by Jane Hawkins, Graphics and maps by Tim Mayer

Published in the United States by Smart Apple Media
1980 Lookout Drive, North Mankato, Minnesota 56003

Printed in Hong Kong

Library of Congress Cataloging-in-Publication Data

Marchant, Kerena. Muhammad and Islam / by Kerena Marchant. p. cm (Great religious leaders)
Summary: An introduction to the religion of Islam and to its prophet, Muhammad.
ISBN 1-58340-217-9
1. Muhammad, Prophet, d. 632 Juvenile literature. 2. Muslims Saudi
Arabia Biography Juvenile literature. [1. Muhammad, Prophet. d 632. 2. Prophets. 3.
Islam.] I. Title. II. Series.
BP75 .M175 2002   297 dc21   2002023120

9 8 7 6 5 4 3 2 1

Cover top: Arabic calligraphy showing the name of Muhammad ﷺ.
Cover main: Pilgrims on hajj circle the Ka'bah at Makkah.
Title page: Muslims celebrate the festival of *Maulud-an-Nabi* in Lamu, Kenya.

Picture Acknowledgements: The publisher would like to thank the following for permission to reproduce their pictures:
Art Directors and Trip Photo Library 8, 12, 15 (top) (H Rogers), 15 (bottom) (Ibrahim), 18 (H Rogers), 24, 31 (H Rogers), 36;
Bridgeman Art Library 11, 13; Britstock-IFA *title page* (Peter Sanders), 4 (Beckwith/Fisher), 5 (bottom) (Hinata Haga), 28 (Peter Sanders), 29 (Kazuyoshi Nomachi), 30 (top) (Kazuyoshi Nomachi), 30 (bottom) (Peter Sanders), 32 (Peter Sanders), 34, 35 (Peter Sanders), 37 (Peter Sanders), 38 (Kazuyoshi Nomachi); Eye Ubiquitous 41 (Bennett Dean), 43 (Julia Waterlow); Impact 6 (David S. Silverberg), 7 (John Cole), 40 (Mark Henley); Peter Sanders *cover top, cover main*, 5 (top), 14, 19, 20, 21, 22, 23, 25, 27, 33 (top), 33 (bottom), 39 (bottom), 42, 44, 45; Hodder Wayland Picture Library 16 (Gordon Clements), 17, 21 (Jim Holmes), 26 (Gordon Clements), 39 (Paul Kenward).

Contents

What Is Islam?

Muslims believe that at the beginning of time there was One God who created all things. He also created Islam as a belief and as a way of life. Muslims believe that Adam ﷺ, the first man, was the first person to believe in the One God and was therefore the first Muslim.

Muslims stop whatever they are doing to pray, five times a day. This means that they think of God throughout the day. ▼

Islam means "submission." It also means "being at peace." Muslims say that there is only the One God, Allah, and they submit their lives to Him. By following Islam, they are at peace with God, themselves, and their fellow Muslims. To live an Islamic life, Muslims closely follow the teachings in the Qur'an, their holy book, and the example of the last Prophet, Muhammad ﷺ.

THE ﷺ SYMBOL

This symbol means *Sallallahu alaihi wa sallam* and is made from the Arabic script of this saying. In English, this means "the peace and blessings of Allah be upon him." Muslims use this after the name of Muhammad ﷺ and all the other Prophets ﷺ as a mark of respect. These words or the symbol are put after the Prophets' ﷺ names in writing, or the words are said after the names are spoken.

The Muslim Prophets ﷺ

The Muslim Prophets ﷺ are people whom God sent to tell others how to live and worship Him. Many of these Prophets ﷺ are also in the Jewish Torah and Christian Bible: for example, Adam ﷺ, Ibrahim (Abraham) ﷺ, Isma'il (Ishmael) ﷺ, Yusuf (Joseph) ﷺ, Musa (Moses) ﷺ, Dawud (David) ﷺ, Sulaiman (Solomon) ﷺ, and Isa (Jesus) ﷺ.

▲ The ﷺ symbol written in Arabic script.

Muhammad ﷺ was a family man, and family values are important to Muslims. ▼

Muhammad, the Prophet ﷺ

Muhammad ﷺ was the last of the Prophets ﷺ and is called the "Prophet of Islam." God revealed the Qur'an to Muhammad ﷺ. By following the Qur'an, Muslims know how God wants them to live and how to lead good lives. Then, if God allows, they can enter Paradise when they die. Islam governs every aspect of life, worship, and the family. It affects everything in life: even eating, drinking, and washing.

The Life of Muhammad ﷺ

In the city of Makkah, there was a man called Abd al Muttalib, who worshipped the One God. Abd al Muttalib had a son, who was married to a woman called Aminah. Aminah was expecting a baby, but just before the baby was due, Abd al Muttalib's son died. A baby boy was born, and Al Muttalib spent a week trying to name him. Eventually, he dreamt that the child should be called Muhammad ﷺ, which means "the praised one." Aminah had had the same dream, and so the baby was named Muhammad ﷺ.

Sadly, Aminah died when Muhammad ﷺ was only six years old, and he became an orphan. Abd al Muttalib, his grandfather, cared for him but soon died too. Muhammad ﷺ, who was only eight at the time, went to work for his uncle as a shepherd. Later, when he was older, his uncle realized he could trust him and called him Al Amin, which means "the trustworthy" or "the truthful one." He gave Muhammad ﷺ a job on his camel trains. This job meant that he could travel to different countries and learn about life there.

◄ The life of the Prophet ﷺ is never illustrated with pictures of him. Islamic art uses clever patterns and Arabic writings based on the message he gave.

THE KA'BAH

The Ka'bah is the monument to the One God. It is a cube-shaped structure in the center of the grand mosque in Makkah. Some people say it was built by the Prophet Adam ﷺ, while others say Ibrahim ﷺ built it. It was restored by the later Prophets ﷺ, Ibrahim ﷺ and Isma'il ﷺ. These Prophets ﷺ believed in the One God. However, after these Prophets ﷺ died, people forgot their teachings about the One God. When Muhammad ﷺ was born, the Ka'bah had no fewer than 360 altars to different gods around it.

When Muhammad ﷺ was 25 years old, he went to work for a wealthy businesswoman called Khadijah, who was 40. She admired Muhammad ﷺ because he was trustworthy, religious, and did not drink alcohol, unlike the other men in Makkah. She asked him to marry her. Despite the age gap, Muhammad ﷺ admired the shrewd businesswoman and had fallen in love with her. They were married and had a family of six children: two sons, who died young, and four daughters.

Many of the people in Makkah did not like having daughters. Muhammad ﷺ, though, loved his daughters and cared for them. He would often take them to pray with him, and all of them, especially his youngest daughter, Fatimah, became true worshippers of the One God.

The Last Prophet

Muhammad ※ felt close to the One God. He was constantly trying to know better what God wanted of him and how he should live his life.

He did not like the way other people in Makkah lived. They worshipped idols, and made money out of selling statues and animals for sacrifice. Many people got drunk and behaved badly. Women were often treated worse than slaves. Muhammad ※ knew this was not the way that God wanted people to live.

One night, when Muhammad ※ was alone in a cave on Mount Hira, the Angel Jibril appeared and told him to read from a roll of silk with letters of fire. Muhammad ※ could not read, and three times he said he could not recite the letters. But suddenly, he felt he knew in his heart what the letters said, and he began to recite some words. These words are now known as the 96th *surah* of the Qur'an.

SURAH

A *surah* is a chapter or section of the Qur'an. There are 114 *surahs* in all.

This is part of the 96th *surah*:

"Recite! In the name of your Lord and Sustainer who created man from a clot of congealed blood, speak those words aloud! Your Lord is the most Generous One—He who has taught the Pen, who reveals directly things far beyond human knowledge."

Muhammad ﷺ was shocked, and he staggered home to Khadijah. He told her what had happened. He was frightened that he might have been tricked by the Devil into thinking he had had a revelation from God. Khadijah knew that her husband was speaking the truth. She became the first person to recognize him as a Prophet of God.

In the years that followed, Muhammad ﷺ had more revelations. Eventually, he was told by God to talk about these messages in public. Muhammad ﷺ spoke out against the idol worshippers and the way people lived in Makkah. Some people agreed with him, but others realized that his teaching would keep them from making money in sales of idols and alcohol. Muhammad ﷺ and his followers were persecuted.

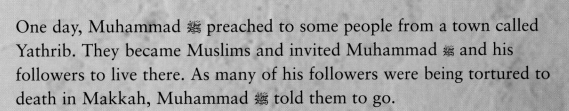

One day, Muhammad ﷺ preached to some people from a town called Yathrib. They became Muslims and invited Muhammad ﷺ and his followers to live there. As many of his followers were being tortured to death in Makkah, Muhammad ﷺ told them to go.

Finally, Muhammad ﷺ left Makkah too. He believed it was the will of God that he establish a Muslim state in Yathrib rather than be killed by the people of Makkah.

The Hijrah and the Jihad

Many people in Makkah hated Muhammad ﷺ. He had to leave, or he would be killed. One night, he escaped with his friend, Abu Bakr.

They were followed by assassins, but they hid in a cave where God protected them. A spider spun a web and a bird built a nest over the entrance. The assassins were convinced that nobody was in the cave. After four days, the Prophet ﷺ and Abu Bakr left the cave and travelled under the cover of night, sleeping by day, to Yathrib. The Prophet ﷺ was riding his unusual white camel, Al Qaswa. This journey is now known as the *Hijrah*.

The people of Yathrib were watching out for them, and when they saw them coming, they lined the streets to welcome them. Everybody wanted Muhammad ﷺ to live with them. Eventually, the Prophet's ﷺ camel stopped by a barn, and there the Prophet ﷺ decided to live and build the first mosque.

Yathrib became known as al-Madinah. There Muhammad ﷺ led the people according to the law that God revealed to him. Everyone lived simply and centered their lives around God. Even though he was the ruler, the Prophet ﷺ led a simple life, growing his crops, feeding his animals, repairing his clothes, and milking his goats. All the people tried to be equal, and servants were well looked after. Women were respected. The Jews who lived in the city were allowed to practice their own beliefs.

However, the people of Makkah still hated Muhammad ﷺ. When a few Muslims raided a Makkahn camel train, the Makkahns decided to attack al-Madinah. The Prophet ﷺ raised an army to fight them. This army was victorious, but in the years that followed, there were other battles, one of which the Muslims lost.

The people of al-Madinah were the first community to center their lives around God and Islam. Their mosque was built at the center of the city. ▼

JIHAD (HOLY WAR)

It was revealed by God to Muhammad ﷺ that war was acceptable if the war was God's will and if it was fought to defend the faith. This is a jihad, or Holy War. Anybody who died in a jihad, fighting for Islam, would go straight to Paradise. Muhammad ﷺ did not allow his army to attack the sick or people who were not fighting. He forbade them to raid houses, to steal, or to destroy fields and farms.

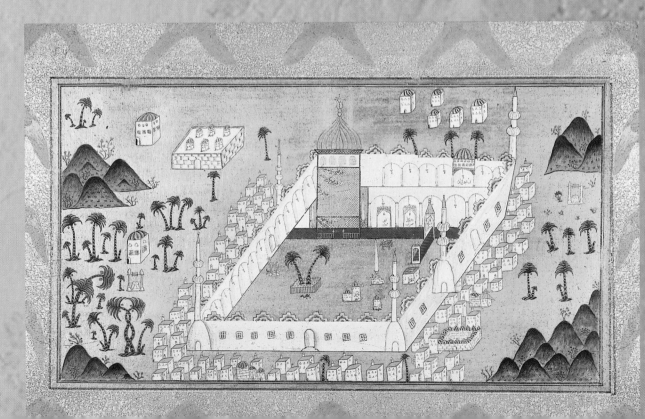

The Return to Makkah

About eight years later, the Prophet took an army of 10,000 men to Makkah. Muhammad led them, riding his white camel and carrying a black banner proclaiming the One God. When the army reached Makkah, only a few people resisted them, and the Prophet rode to the Ka'bah. There he dismounted, circled the Ka'bah seven times, and touched the sacred black stone. The idols were destroyed. At midday, Muhammad called everyone to prayer.

Makkah had been conquered, and only 11 people were killed. The Makkahns returned to the worship of the One God. Muhammad forgave his enemies, and soon everybody in Makkah became Muslims. It was forbidden for non-Muslims to enter the city or live there. The Prophet then returned to al-Madinah.

Two years later, the Prophet returned to Makkah on a pilgrimage. More than 100,000 people joined him, and he preached a great sermon that summarized all the messages God had revealed to him. He ended by saying, "Have I fulfilled my mission?" The crowd roared, "You have fulfilled it, O Messenger of God!" Everybody then prayed.

The Prophet returned to al-Madinah. There he became ill with a fever and headaches. He was too ill to leave his bed and pray with his people, but he prayed from his deathbed. Finally, he lay back, exhausted, saying, "God, grant me pardon." After that, he died.

◀ A Persian drawing of the Ka'bah at Makkah and the Prophet's mosque at al-Madinah.

Many of his followers refused to believe that the Prophet ﷺ was dead. Abu Bakr, the prophet's friend, reminded them that Muhammad ﷺ was a person and must not be worshipped, just remembered as the last of the Prophets ﷺ, the Messengers of God.

"Muhammad ﷺ is but a messenger; there have been many prophets before him, and they all died. If he dies or is killed, will you now turn back?"

Qur'an

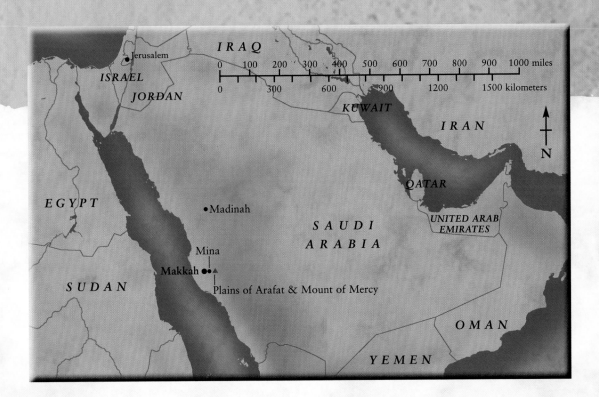

WHO WAS THE LEADER?

After Muhammad ﷺ died, scribes wrote down everything he did or said. He was born in 569 C.E. in the city of Makkah, which is in present-day Saudi Arabia. He was a member of the powerful Quraish tribe, who were the most important tribe in the city. In 610, he

▲ Makkah and al-Madinah are located in present-day Saudi Arabia.

had his first revelation from God. In 622, he emigrated from Makkah to al-Madinah, where he established the first Muslim state. He died on June 8, 632, at the age of 63.

Muhammad ﷺ Teaches God's Message

There Is Only One God

Muhammad's ﷺ teaching was not his own: it was God's because it came directly from God. This teaching covers all aspects of life: a person's relationship with God, relationship to others, family life, and everyday life.

▲ Saudi Arabia, the modern-day country which contains Makkah and al-Madinah, is proud of its Islamic faith. It uses the *Shahadah* on its national flag.

All Muslims believe in the One God, Allah. God is at the center of their lives in everything they do. Each morning and night, Muslims say the *Shahadah*, the Muslim profession of faith: *"I witness that there is no God but Allah, and that Muhammad ﷺ is the prophet of Allah."*

The Greatness of God

To Muslims, God is so great, He is beyond their imagination. In the Qur'an, there are no fewer than 99 names and ways of describing the greatness of God.

Muslims forbid pictures of God, as well as of the Prophets ﷺ. This is because God is so great and has no form so He cannot be compared to any created thing without being misrepresented. The only way to worship God is by following His true teachings in the Qur'an.

Prayer

Muslims pray five times per day. This act of worship ensures that they stop whatever they are doing throughout the day to put God first. It also helps them to remain close to God in between prayers and to remember their faith because they build their routine around it.

Life after death

In the Qur'an, Muslims are reminded that because God is merciful, there is life after death. To enter Paradise, people have to live good lives centered around God. After death, God will ask each person about his or her life and decide whether he or she should go to Paradise or Hell. Nobody can assume that he will enter Paradise; only God can decide.

▲ A poster showing the 99 names of Allah.

THE FIVE PILLARS OF ISLAM

Muhammad ﷺ wanted to ensure that Muslims put God at the very center of their lives and gave them five duties, known as the Five Pillars of Islam. The five duties are:

- The Muslim profession of faith, the *Shahadah* (see page 14)
- Praying five times a day, to put God at the center of their lives
- Fasting, to be grateful for the gifts of God
- The giving of charity, to remind them that everything belongs to God
- Going on pilgrimage (hajj) to Makkah once in a lifetime, if they can afford it after carrying out all their family duties.

▲ A Saudi Muslim gives out aid from Saudi Arabia to Muslims affected by the civil war in Bosnia.

All Muslims Are Equal

The *Ummah* is the worldwide Muslim community or "nation of Muhammad 🕮." Muslims believe they are equal in the eyes of God and are united by their belief in the One God.

These Muslims in Pakistan remember the One God at Friday prayers. All over the world, Muslims pray using the same language, Arabic. ▼

United Muslims

The idea of people being united in this way was unheard of before Muhammad's 🕮 time. The different Arab tribes were only loyal to each other and were constantly fighting. Any person who was not a member of a tribe was no better than a slave. To unite all these people and give them one belief and one way of life was one of Muhammad's 🕮 greatest achievements. Muhammad 🕮 encouraged Muslims to respect each other and not to kill, wage war, or steal from each other.

Everyone is equal

One way Muhammad 🕮 united Muslims was by insisting that all Muslims see their five duties as ways of being equal with each other. Five times a day, all Muslims all over the world from all classes pray to One God as equals. During the fast, and by the giving of charity, the gap between the rich and the poor is narrowed. On the hajj (pilgrimage to Makkah), all the pilgrims wear similar white robes, and all barriers of class and nationality disappear.

Islam and money

One of the strongest messages Muhammad ﷺ preached was that money must not divide Muslims. He reminded Muslims that everything they had came from God in trust. Therefore, every Muslim has to give two-fifths of his or her income to charity. It is forbidden to charge interest on loans. Employers must make sure their servants are well fed and clothed.

Muslim women are respected both in the home, where they are the center of family life, and at work. Many women, such as this nurse, hold professional jobs. ▼

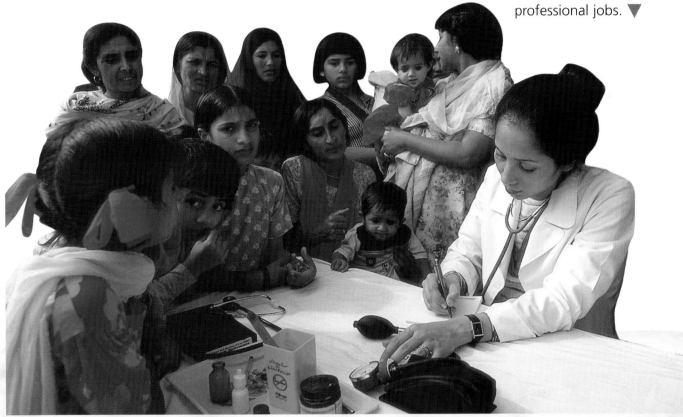

WOMEN AND ISLAM

Muhammad ﷺ grew up in a society where women were not always respected. Female babies were often killed at birth, and women were treated as slaves with no rights whatsoever. The rules in the Qur'an that govern how women should be treated and dress are designed to give them a role, protect them, and give them respect.

"People, your wives have a certain right over you, and you have certain rights over them. Treat them well and be kind to them, for they are your partners and committed helpers."

Hadith

The Family

A man came to the Prophet Muhammad ✿ and asked him who was entitled to be treated best. The Prophet ✿ replied, "Your mother." The man asked, "Then who?" and the Prophet ✿ again replied, "Your mother." The man again asked, and the Prophet ✿ said, "Your father."

Hadith

Family life is the cornerstone of Islam. Muslims look to the example of Muhammad's ✿ family, particularly to the example of his wife, Khadijah, and daughter, Fatimah. Muslims believe that people are born Muslims, but that the family determines whether they are true Muslims.

Mothers

The home is central to Islam, and it is a mother's domain. It should be clean, and there should be prayer mats in readiness for prayer. The right food should be prepared (see page 20). In the Arab world, there is a saying: "The mother is a school." A mother teaches her children about Islam.

A mother leads her children in the traditional prayers before a meal. ▼

SAYING THE ADHAN TO A BABY

As soon as a Muslim baby is born, the first words he or she will hear are the *Adhan*, the call to prayer. This has special meaning for Muslims, as it means that the first words the baby hears are about the One God and the relationship, as a Muslim, to God. They hope that the child will grow up living a Muslim life. As soon as the baby is born, one of the parents will whisper the words in the baby's right ear.

Allah is most great!
Allah is most great!
I testify that there is no God but Allah.
I testify that Muhammad ﷺ is the Messenger of Allah.
Come to prayer.
Come to salvation.
God is great.
There is no God besides Allah.

After this, they will whisper the *iqamah*, the call to stand up for prayers, in the baby's left ear.

▲ Whispering the *Adhan* to a newborn baby. This is part of the commitment that each Muslim father makes to God and to his children.

Throughout the day, she will set an example and teach the children to pray. She will make sure they are clean and have good manners. The children will learn to share what they have with others and to invite friends and neighbors into their homes.

Fathers

A father's main duty is to ensure that his children are well provided for. He will also be a teacher to them, setting a good example. His job is to teach them the ways of the world outside the home. He will also help them to read the Qur'an and take them to mosque.

Children and parents

In all his teaching, Muhammad ﷺ insisted that children must respect their parents and look after them in their old age.

Rules for Everyday Life

As Islam is a way of life, it describes how to perform daily tasks such as washing and eating. These guidelines are either taken from the Qur'an, or from the example set by the Prophet Muhammad in his own life and written in the Hadith.

Keeping clean

Cleanliness is of utmost importance. Muslims wash before they say prayers five times a day and before eating. If they feel dirty at any time, they will wash. There are guidelines in the Qur'an about washing. It must always be in clean running water.

Eating and food

Eating food that is fresh and healthy is also important. Animals have to be killed in a special way that is humane and hygienic. Meat that is killed in this way is called *halal*.

There is usually somewhere to wash at mosques so that everyone can wash before prayers. ▼

▲ Muslims are hospitable people and like to share their food with guests.

Muslims follow Muhammad's ﷺ example by eating with their right hand. They always make sure this hand is clean for eating. ▶

Muslims will only eat meat that has had all the blood drained from it. They will not eat meat that comes from a pig, or from an animal that has died naturally or been killed in an accident.

Table manners are also important. At every meal, enough food is prepared for the family and anyone who might call in. Children must never begin a meal before their parents, and the hosts must wait for their guests to start eating. It is forbidden to talk with food in your mouth.

Muslims should begin their meal with the word *Bismillah*—"in the name of God"—and say *al-hamdu-li-Llah*—"praise God"—when finished.

ISLAMIC LAW: SHARI'AH

Islamic countries base their laws on the rules laid down by the Qur'an and the example set by the Prophet ﷺ in the Hadith. This law is called the *Shari'ah* or "path."

"This is my straight path, so follow it, and do not follow paths which will separate you from this path."

Qur'an

For example, Westerners in some Muslim countries, such as Saudi Arabia, must follow the *Shari'ah*. If they disobey, they face a public beating or prison.

The Sacred Texts

Al Qur'an

Al Qur'an means "that which should be read." It is the word of God and tells people how to lead good lives, submitting themselves to the will of God. It also tells of the creation of the world, of various Prophets ﷺ, and of the history of religion.

▲ Copying this 18th-century Qur'an would have been a labor of love for a calligrapher, and have taken many months to complete.

The Qur'an was revealed to Muhammad ﷺ over a period of 23 years. During the month of *Ramadan*, Muhammad ﷺ would recite everything he had been told to ensure that he did not forget anything. Today, Muslims want to be like the Prophet ﷺ and memorize the Qur'an. People who know the Qur'an by heart are called *hafiz*.

"I leave behind me two things, the Qur'an and my example, and if you follow these you will not fail."

Hadith

Writing down the Qur'an

During the early persecution of Muslims, many *hafiz* were killed in battle, and Abu Bakr, the Prophet's ﷺ friend, was concerned that all the people who could remember the Qur'an might die. He asked the Prophet's ﷺ secretary, Zaid ibn Thabit, to make a book of all the revelations the Prophet ﷺ had received. About 18 years after the death of the Prophet ﷺ, in 650 C.E., Zaid collected the verses from those who remained from the Prophet's ﷺ time and carefully wrote them down on whatever he could find: pieces of leather, paper, palm leaves, and stones. They were then copied into a book.

▲ Many Muslims read the Qur'an on a stand as a mark of respect to the precious word of God.

A gift from God

The Qur'an is the most beautiful Arabic poetry. The Prophet ﷺ, who probably could not read or write very well, would not have written this himself. Muslims believe that it is the most beautiful gift they have from God.

Muslims treat the Qur'an with great respect. They always wash before touching it. While it is being read, nobody makes a noise or eats. They are careful not to touch it unnecessarily and usually place it on a special stool called a *kursi* or a stand called a *rihil* to read it. When it is not being read, it is sometimes kept in a cover on the highest shelf with nothing on top of it.

THE QUR'AN

The Qur'an is not written down in the order that Muhammad ﷺ received the revelations. The longest chapter comes first and the shorter chapters last. And all chapters, except one, begin the same way: "In the name of Allah, the most merciful, the most kind."

The Inspiration of the Qur'an

Calligraphy

The Qur'an is the inspiration for all Islamic art. Copying the beautiful verses of the Qur'an, which are the word of God, had to be done well. Scribes who copied the Qur'an by hand developed the art of calligraphy or decorative handwriting. Muhammad could not write himself, but he encouraged calligraphy and said, "Good writing makes the truth stand out."

Because Muslims are forbidden to draw pictures of people or animals, verses from the Qur'an are used to decorate mosques. All over mosques you can see verses from the Qur'an written beautifully and imaginatively, reminding worshippers of the word of God. The most copied section of the Qur'an is the opening chapter, the al-Fatihah.

Qur'anic calligraphy has also been used to decorate Muslim homes. Plates are decorated with verses praising God—another way for God to be in all parts of a Muslim's life.

"If the ocean became ink for transcribing the words of God, surely the ocean would be exhausted before the words of my Lord came to an end."

Qur'an

This man has spent years learning to embroider Qur'anic verses in gold to make the giant cloth called the *Kiswah* that is used to cover the Ka'bah in Makkah. It takes a team of weavers a year to make the *Kiswah,* which is replaced every year. ▼

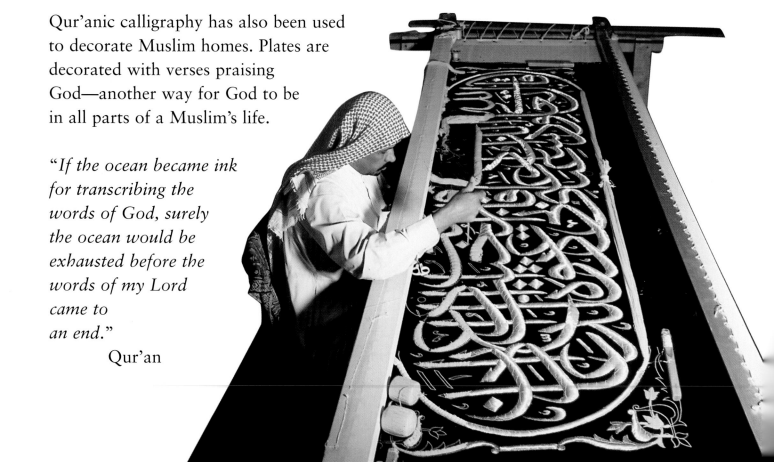

▲ A Qur'anic recitation competition for school children in Lamu Island, Kenya.

Reading and storytelling

Muslims do not read the Qur'an in any language other than Arabic, if they can help it, so that the word of God is always pure and beautiful. It is a form of art to recite the Qur'an and bring out the poetry. At Muslim festivals, people travel many miles to hear the Qur'an performed by a famous reciter, and there are Qur'anic recitation competitions.

Muslims love storytelling. However, they have to be careful when they tell stories from the Qur'an, in case they change the story or the meaning. The story must be the same as it is in the Qur'an. Nothing must be changed because the Qur'an is the word of God.

THE AL-FATIHAH
The opening verses of the Qur'an are:
"In the name of Allah, Most Gracious, Most Merciful.
Praise be to Allah, Lord of the Worlds,
The Most Gracious, the Most Merciful;
Master of the Day of Judgement.
You alone we worship and You alone we ask for help.
Guide us on the straight way, the way of those You have favored,
Not the path of those who earn your anger, nor of those who go astray."

The Sunnah

The Prophet Muhammad ﷺ set an example of how
Muslims should live with both his words and his actions.
Everything that has been collected about the Prophet ﷺ—
what he did and said, and stories about his life—is called
the *Sunnah*. The *Sunnah* contains the Hadith, which is a
collection of sayings by the Prophet ﷺ, and the *Sirah*,
which is his biography.

The Hadith

Because Muhammad ﷺ could not write anything down,
trusted scribes carefully wrote everything down that he
said or did. Eventually, all these reports were collected
together to form the Hadith. Each Hadith was carefully
checked to ensure that it was an accurate account of what
the Prophet ﷺ did or said. When each Hadith was written
down, it contained a list of the people who passed on the
saying, to prove that it was genuine.

Learning to read the Qur'an at a
mosque school in Pakistan. Many
of these boys will know the
Qur'an by heart by the time they
have grown up. ▼

TREATMENT OF ANIMALS

The accounts of Muhammad's ☆ life show him to be an animal lover. The kindness he showed to everybody was also extended to animals. One night, when he went to sleep, using his only cloak as a blanket, he woke up the next morning to find that a cat and her kittens were asleep in his cloak. He then cut off the corner they were sleeping on so they should not be disturbed.

The teachings of the Hadith come from God, but they are not the direct word of God, unlike the Qur'an. It is therefore possible to discuss them in a way that Muslims would not discuss the Qur'an.

There are two kinds of Hadith. The sacred Hadith are sayings that God revealed to Muhammad ☆, but they are not in the Qur'an. These sayings are treated with the greatest of reverence. The prophetic Hadith are the words and sayings of Muhammad ☆, which show him to be a God-fearing and compassionate man.

One of the messages to come from the Hadith is about caring for the earth. God made people the protectors of the planet and of all life. Humans must show love and compassion to all living creatures.

"If someone kills a sparrow for sport, the sparrow will cry out on the Day of Judgement, 'O, Lord, that person did not kill me for any useful sport.'"

Hadith

▲ There is little for these calves to graze on, but their owner will do his best to feed them and care for them.

The Sacred Places

Makkah

It is the duty of every Muslim to go on hajj to Makkah at least once in his or her lifetime as commanded in the Qur'an. The only people who are excused from this duty are those who are too old, sick, disabled, or poor to afford to go.

The Ka'bah

Makkah, which is in present-day Saudi Arabia, is the Muslims' most sacred city. Muslims believe that the city is directly under the throne of Allah, and some believe that here Adam ﷺ first built a monument to the One God. This monument was later destroyed in the great flood of biblical times, but was rebuilt by the prophets Ibrahim ﷺ and Isma'il ﷺ. The Ka'bah houses a black stone from Heaven which the Angel Jibril gave to Ibrahim ﷺ and Isma'il ﷺ. It was the Prophet Muhammad ﷺ who banned idol worship in Makkah and returned the Ka'bah to the worship of the One God.

The Hajj

The events of the hajj mark important events in the lives of Adam ﷺ, Ibrahim ﷺ, Isma'il ﷺ, and Muhammad ﷺ. They help to bring the pilgrims closer to God.

◀ The Ka'bah in Makkah is the most sacred place in the world to Muslims.

The pilgrims wear white clothes called *ihram*. The men wear two plain, white, unsewn cloths and the women a simple white dress. The clothes show the equality and purity of the pilgrims. Pilgrims begin their pilgrimage at the Ka'bah. They circle the Ka'bah seven times in a counter-clockwise direction, starting from the black stone. This sets their mind on God.

Next, they go to the two hills of Marwa and Safa. There Ibrahim ﷺ left his wife, Hajar, and her son, Isma'il ﷺ. Hajar had faith in God to provide for her and her son when her husband left. Hajar soon ran out of food and water and ran between the two hills searching for water. She called upon God, and her faith was rewarded: the Angel Jibril appeared, struck the ground with his wing, and a stream gushed forth. Hajar made the stream into the Well of Zamzam, which is the purest water in the world. Muslims on hajj run or walk between the two hills as Hajar did, and then drink from the well.

▲ Pilgrims leave Makkah for the Plains of Arafat with only their copies of the Qur'an, water to drink, and umbrellas for shade.

The Plains of Arafat

After visiting all the sites in or near Makkah, about two million pilgrims travel to the Plains of Arafat, where a huge campsite is erected. It was here, on the Mount of Mercy, that Adam ﷺ and Eve stood before God to be forgiven. It was also here that the Prophet Muhammad ﷺ preached his last sermon. Here the pilgrims stand before God as Adam ﷺ and Eve did and pray and reflect.

Mina

After this, they travel to Mina. In the old town of Mina are three pillars. These represent the devils who tempted Ibrahim ﷺ to disobey God's command to sacrifice his son, Isma'il ﷺ. Just as Ibrahim ﷺ, Isma'il ﷺ, and Hajar drove away these devils with stones, the pilgrims throw stones at the pillars to symbolize their rejection of evil. If they miss, they have to repeat the throw.

▲ Millions of pilgrims stand from noon to sunset on and around the Mount of Mercy.

Throwing stones at a pillar in Mina. ▼

THE FIRST HAJJ

The hajj began when the Prophet Ibrahim ﷺ finished rebuilding the Ka'bah and God commanded him to call people to pilgrimage there. Ibrahim ﷺ climbed on to the top of a nearby mountain, worried that nobody would hear him call them to come on hajj, but God relayed Ibrahim's ﷺ call far and wide, and people obeyed the command.

Id-ul-Adha

The hajj ends with the feast of *Id-ul-Adha*. This festival recalls how Ibrahim ﷺ obeyed God's command to sacrifice his son Isma'il ﷺ, and how God, in His mercy, spared Isma'il ﷺ by putting a ram in his place. Pilgrims change into ordinary clothes and celebrate the festival. Muslims who do not go on hajj also celebrate this festival.

This house in Egypt has been decorated with pictures of the hajj as a reminder of the pilgrimage. ▼

MALCOLM X

Malcolm X, the American black civil rights leader, visited Makkah on hajj. In the U.S., he was not treated equally by white people. On hajj, he was moved by the equality of the pilgrims in their *ihram* clothes, whatever their race, color, or class.

"They were of all colors, from blue-eyed blondes to Black Africans. But we were all participating in the same ritual, displaying a sense of unity and brotherhood that my experiences in America had led me to believe never could exist between the white and non-white."

al-Madinah

After their pilgrimage to Makkah, many pilgrims visit al-Madinah, 80 miles (125 km) away, which is Islam's second holiest city. On the visit to al-Madinah, Muslims reflect more on the example set by the Prophet ﷺ. However, they do not worship him or see him as anything other than a good and wise man whose example is worth following. Muslims believe that nothing must distract anybody from worshipping God.

Mosques

Present day al-Madinah is very different from the simple city where the Prophet ﷺ lived. All the places that are connected with him are now beautiful, elaborate mosques with elegant minarets and beautiful calligraphy.

There are a number of sites to visit. There is the simple al-Quba mosque, which stands on the site where

The Prophet's ﷺ Mosque at al-Madinah. This is where Muhammad ﷺ and his close friends are buried. It was originally the simple home of the Prophet ﷺ, but over the centuries it has become more and more elaborate as different rulers have added to it. ▼

Muhammad's ﷺ camel, al Qaswa, rested and the first mosque was built. The Qiblatain mosque is different from all other mosques. It has two *Qiblahs*, the part of the mosque that Muslims face when they pray. *Qiblahs* almost always face Makkah. However, in this mosque, one faces Makkah and one faces Jerusalem (see page 34).

There is also the grand Prophet's ﷺ Mosque, with its four lovely minarets, which is built on the site of the Prophet's ﷺ simple home. Inside is the tomb of Muhammad ﷺ and those of his close friends, who became the Muslim leaders after his death. The sealed doors of the Prophet's ﷺ tomb have this inscription, which sets out Muhammad's ﷺ role:

"There is none to worship but God, the Rightful and True Lord. Muhammad ﷺ is God's Messenger and the faithful attester of the certain promise."

▲ The Prophet's ﷺ tomb is adorned with beautiful metal and ornate woodwork.

Fatimah's simple grave in the Baqia graveyard. ▼

FATIMAH'S GRAVE

Some Muslims gain inspiration from the lives of the Prophet's ﷺ family, and a visit to al-Madinah is a chance to visit their simple graves. One of these belongs to Fatimah, the Prophet's ﷺ daughter. Fatimah was the only child of the Prophet ﷺ to give him grandchildren. She went with her father to many battles, and her example as a woman and mother is followed by many women. She only survived her father by three months, dying young at the age of 30.

Jerusalem

Jerusalem is the third most holy city in Islam after Makkah and al-Madinah. In the early years, all Muslims faced Jerusalem when they prayed. Eventually, the Prophet ﷺ changed this, after a revelation from God, to Makkah, the city of the Ka'bah, the monument to the One God.

The Temple to the One God

Jerusalem is said to be the place where Ibrahim ﷺ was ordered by God to sacrifice his son Isma'il ﷺ. It is also where the sacred law, given by God to the Muslim Prophet Musa ﷺ (Moses), was kept. Both Dawud ﷺ and Sulaiman ﷺ built the Temple to the One God there. It is also where the Muslim Prophet Isa ﷺ (Jesus) preached his message.

▲ The Dome of the Rock was built on the site of the original Temple of the One God in Jerusalem.

Muhammad's footprints

According to the Hadith, Muhammad flew on a winged horse from Makkah to the Temple in Jerusalem. There he climbed up a ladder to Heaven, where he met all the Prophets who had gone before him. He also negotiated with God, with the help of Musa, over how many times a day people should pray. It was finally set at five times a day. There are marks on the rock, which are reported to be the Prophet's footprints as he ascended into Heaven.

The history of the Temple site

After the Prophet's death, Muslim warriors captured Palestine, the country around Jerusalem. The Christian ruler of Jerusalem refused to hand over the city unless Umar, one of the Prophet's friends and the current Muslim leader, personally accepted his surrender. Umar came into Jerusalem and was shocked to see that the Temple had fallen down and was used as a rubbish dump. Umar began to clear the rubble himself and eventually uncovered the site where the Prophet ascended into Heaven. With his own hands, he built a wooden mosque over the site. Later, this was replaced with the beautiful Dome of the Rock mosque, with its glorious golden dome covering the sacred rock.

OTHER RELIGIONS IN JERUSALEM

When the early Muslims conquered countries such as Palestine, they respected the Christians and Jews and allowed them to practice their beliefs. They realized that they worshipped the One God and acknowledged the Prophets.

"Their churches shall not be taken away nor shall they be forced to give up their beliefs nor shall they be persecuted for them."

Contract made between Umar and the Christians of Jerusalem.

The sacred rock is housed inside the Dome of the Rock building. ▼

Special Occasions

Festivals

The Arabic word for festival is *id,* which means "to return at regular intervals." Muslims see festivals as a time to praise God and remember the life of the Prophets ﷺ. They are a time to make a fresh start and catch up with friends. During festivals, Muslims will make sure that everyone can join in the celebrations. They will take care to see that the poor have enough food and that people who might be on their own have company.

▲ A festival feast prepared for the poor at a mosque in Kashmir.

Muharram

This is the first month of the Muslim calendar. It starts with the Muslim new year's day called *Al Hijrah*. This is the anniversary of the emigration (*Hijra*) of Muhammad ﷺ and his followers from Makkah to al-Madinah. In the Christian calendar, this took place in 622, but in the Muslim calendar this year is A.H. 1, the first year after the *Hijra*. For Muslims, this was a very important event, as it saw the first community that was ruled according to the law of God as set out in the Qur'an.

All over the world, Muslims commemorate the new year by telling stories about the Prophet ﷺ and by extra night-time prayers. It is also a time to start life afresh.

However, *Muharram* is also the month in which almost all of the Prophet's ﷺ descendants were killed. Some Muslims mourn during this month with processions, beating their breasts and lamenting loudly.

Maulud-an-Nabi (Prophet's ﷺ birthday)

This celebration takes place on the 12th day of *Rabi'ul-Awwal*, the third month of the year. This is a festival that was not set up in the Qur'an or introduced by the Prophet ﷺ in the Hadith. Some strict Muslims do not celebrate it, as they believe that it is hero worship.

The majority of Muslims do celebrate it in style. There are processions through the town, and crowds will gather to hear stories about the Prophet ﷺ. People will also sing songs called *naat*, which are about the Prophet ﷺ and the example he set.

THE ISLAMIC CALENDAR

The Muslim calendar is a lunar calendar. Each of the 12 months in the Muslim calendar begins with the new moon. The Christian calendar is based on the sun. As lunar months are shorter than solar months, the Muslim calendar is 11 days shorter than the Christian calendar. Festivals, therefore, occur 11 days earlier each year as compared to the Christian calendar.

◄ *Maulud* processions take place all over the world, even in non-Muslim countries such as Britain.

Ramadan

The ninth month of the Muslim calendar, *Ramadan*, is a special month for Muslims. It was during this month that the Qur'an was revealed to the Prophet Muhammad ﷺ. This is marked by fasting each day during *Ramadan*, from sunrise to sunset.

The Qur'an is divided into 30 sections, and Muslims aim to read all of the Qur'an during this month. The Night of Power, which falls around the 26th day of *Ramadan*, is the night that the Qur'an was first given to Muhammad ﷺ. This event is marked by readings of the Qur'an in mosques that go on into the night.

▲ Muslim pilgrims at the Prophet's ﷺ Mosque at al-Madinah join together for the *iftar* meal that breaks the daily fast. The Prophet ﷺ and his followers would have eaten a similar meal there centuries ago.

Muslims don't find fasting a hardship. Instead, they feel that it brings them closer to God and to others. Because *Ramadan* occurs 11 days earlier each year, the fast can occur in different seasons. In winter, Muslims may have to go through a cold day without warm food or drink, and in the heat of summer have nothing to drink. The only people who are excused from fasting are young children and people who are travelling or too sick.

"O ye who believe!
Fasting is prescribed to you
As it was prescribed
To those before you
That ye may learn
self restraint."

Qur'an

Id-ul-Fitr

Ramadan ends with the festival of *Id-ul-Fitr*. It begins with prayers, and then the festivities begin, at home and around the mosque. Presents and cards are exchanged, and families and friends come together for feasting. There are Qur'an reciting competitions in many countries.

▲ Everybody wears their best clothes at *Id-ul-Fitr*. This Muslim family lives in Kenya.

A man gives *zakat* after praying at a mosque in England. ▼

ZAKAT-UL-FITR

Every Muslim has to pay *Zakat-ul-Fitr* to the mosque at the end of *Ramadan*. This is so that the mosque can make sure that there is enough food to eat at *Id* for everybody, even the very poor. Any money that is left over is used for other charity work. In Indonesia, the government collects the *zakat*.

Zakat, the giving of charity, is one of the Five Pillars of Islam. Muslims do not expect any reward for it. Giving *zakat* is cleansing, as it frees Muslims from any attachments to wealth and money, and reminds them that everything belongs to God.

Id-ul-Adha

"Neither the flesh of the animals of your sacrifice nor their blood reach Allah—it is your righteousness that reaches Him."

Qur'an

Id-ul-Adha is the most important festival in the Muslim year. This festival occurs during the hajj month and ends the hajj. Muslims not on hajj celebrate the festival at home. *Id-ul-Adha* means "the festival of the sacrifice." Muslims focus on their willingness to give up everything for God if they are called to do so. After all, everything Muslims have is owned by God.

During this festival, Muslims remember how the Prophet Ibrahim was willing to sacrifice his beloved son, Isma'il, to God, and how Isma'il was willing to be sacrificed.

The Qur'an and the Hadith give plenty of instructions about how this festival should be celebrated to ensure that animals are treated well, and that Muslims understand the meaning behind the festival. In non-Western countries where there are no butchers,

Sheep or goats are usually killed at the festival of *Id-ul-Adha* to remember how God, at the last minute, sent a sheep to be sacrificed instead of Isma'il. ▼

every Muslim is taught how to kill an animal so it feels no pain. Muslims follow Muhammad's ﷺ example and believe that they have a duty to be kind to all animals. They find it extremely hard to kill an animal that they have cared for, yet Ibrahim ﷺ was prepared to sacrifice his son. The Qur'an and the Hadith are very clear that Muslims must only kill animals if they need them for food.

The meat from the animal is used to feed the family, and any leftover meat is given to the poor. In some countries, this is the only time that poor people get to eat meat.

"Sacrifice is a selfless offering to God of something that one cherishes and not an attempt to win favors from Him. He is above human needs and human emotions."

Qur'an

"People shouldn't eat meat if they are not prepared to be responsible for killing in the kindest way."

Muslim saying

Muslims always make sure the animal whose meat they are buying has been humanely killed. They will buy meat only from a special *halal* butcher.

Birth and Death

Birth

Muslims believe that everything comes in trust from God, even children, who are gifts from God. After the whispering of the *Adhan*, the call to prayer, to a new baby, there is a naming ceremony. This takes place a week after the baby is born.

Muslims take great care to choose the right names for their children. The most popular name in the world for boys is that of the Prophet Muhammad. Some of the most popular girls' names in the Muslim world are those of the Prophet's beloved wife, Khadijah, and his daughter, Fatimah. Muslims hope that their children will be like the Prophet and his family, and be good Muslims.

▲ A proud father with his baby daughter who has had her hair shaved during her naming ceremony.

When the child is named, the child's hair is shaved off and the weight of the hair in silver or gold is given by some people to the poor. (If a child is bald, the parents may still make a donation.)

Death

Muslims must always be ready for death. They carefully follow the Qur'an and live in submission to the will of God so that God will judge them well when they die.
They see death as a time when they can be close to God. However, no one can assume that he has lived a good life and will enter Paradise. Only God can do that.

A Muslim tries to die in the same way as Muhammad ﷺ. When Muhammad ﷺ knew he was dying, he prayed, "Allah, help me through the hardship and agony of death." He also asked for forgiveness of his sins.

When Muslims die, they follow this example and ask for forgiveness and the blessing of their family and God. They hope that the last word they will hear when they die will be that of God.

Muslim funerals are simple affairs, as Muslims believe that everybody is equal in death. No one is rich or poor, important or humble in death. Every Muslim is buried in a shroud made from white sheets and placed in a grave.

Chinese Muslims visiting a graveyard at *Ramadan*. Each grave is placed so that the body faces Makkah. ▼

Islam in the World Today

Living like Muhammad ﷺ

Muslims look back at Muhammad ﷺ and his Muslim community in al-Madinah as the ideal Muslim state. It was a community of devout Muslims living by the commands of God in the Qur'an. This is the aim of every Muslim and every Muslim country today: to live a good life like the Prophet ﷺ and to be governed by God's law.

▲ Modern Makkah, in Saudi Arabia, is very different from the simple place where Ibrahim ﷺ rebuilt the Ka'bah.

Today, many Muslim countries are governed by Islamic law, but it is much more difficult for them to live like Muhammad ﷺ and his early followers, who were poor people living simple lives. Many Muslim countries are rich from selling oil, which makes it hard to copy the simple values of the people of al-Madinah.

Muslim values

Many non-Muslims argue that, as the Qur'an was written hundreds of years ago, many of its laws are out of date. Some of them believe that Muslim countries need to update their laws.

Most Muslims would argue that this is not the case and that the Qur'an, God's way of life, will always be up to date and must never be changed. There is much to be said for this. The Muslim world is usually united, and there have been few wars between Muslims throughout history.

Mosques are always full, as Islam remains a living, active faith to all who follow it. There are low crime figures in Muslim countries. Shops in countries such as Saudi Arabia remain open and unattended while the owners go for prayers, and nothing is ever stolen. The family is at the center of Muslim life. Women in Muslim countries often wear long robes and veils, but they are rarely attacked in the streets because they are respected.

Non-Muslim countries cannot always boast of these values. Throughout history, people of the same faith have fought each other in wars. Today, Christian countries are not always united because of a shared faith. Western countries have high crime rates, and family values there are not as important as they used to be—proof, perhaps, that the Message of God, as revealed by Muhammad ﷺ, is a message for all times and all places.

Muslims from different backgrounds praying in the desert of Wyoming in the U.S. ▼

THE SPREAD OF ISLAM

In the centuries after the Prophet's ﷺ death, Islam spread all over the Middle East, Africa, Asia, and the Far East. It even spread north into the former USSR and into Eastern Europe. In the 20th century, Islam spread to Britain, Western Europe, and the U.S. as immigrants from Muslim countries went in search of work. Today, Islam is the fastest growing religion in the world, and there are more than one billion Muslims.

Glossary

Adhan The Muslim call to prayer that is chanted before (the five daily) prayers.

al-Fatihah The opening chapter of the Qur'an.

Allah The Arabic word for God.

Angel A being who acts as a messenger between God and human beings, usually prophets.

Assassins People who murder (or who want to murder) someone who is a leader.

Calligraphy Decorative and beautiful handwriting.

Camel train At the time of Muhammad, camels were used by traders to transport goods across the desert.

C.E. "Of the common era."

Devil The supreme spirit of evil.

Hadith The collection of sayings of the Prophet Muhammad.

Hafiz People who can recite the Qur'an by heart.

Hajj The pilgrimage to Makkah that every Muslim who can must make.

Halal An Arabic word that means "allowed" and describes food and drink which is allowed under Islamic law.

Hijrah The emigration of Muhammad and his followers from Makkah to al-Madinah.

Idol A picture or a statue of a god which people worship.

Ihram The white clothes worn by pilgrims on hajj, and the state they are in when they make the pilgrimage.

Iqamah The call to stand up for prayers.

Islam The religion that Muslims follow.

Ka'bah The cube-shaped monument to the One God in Makkah.

Makkah Muslims' most holy city. It is in present-day Saudi Arabia.

Minarets The towers of a mosque.

Mosque The building where Muslims go to pray together.

Muslims People who believe in the One God and the message of the Prophet Muhammad.

Paradise Muslims believe this is a beautiful and peaceful place where good people go after they die.

Persecuted Treated very badly over a long period of time.

Pilgrims People who travel to a holy place for religious reasons.

Prophets People who tell others what God wants.

Qur'an Muslims' holy book, which they believe is the word of God.

Ramadan The month when Muslims fast to commemorate the time that God gave the Qur'an to the Prophet.

Sacrifice Killing an animal as an offering to God.

Shahadah The Muslim declaration of faith in the One God and the Prophet Muhammad.

Sins Bad acts; doing things that are wrong.

Ummah The worldwide Muslim community.

Further Information

Read More

Gordon, Matthew S. *Islam*. New York: Facts on File, 1991.

Khan, Rukhsana. *Muslim Child: Understanding Islam through Stories and Poems*. Morton Grove, Ill.: Albert Whitman & Co., 2002.

Knight, Khadijah. *Islamic Festivals*. Crystal Lake, Ill.: Heinemann Library, 1997.

Langley, Myrtle. *Eyewitness: Religion*. London: Dorling Kindersley Publishing, 2000.

Marston, Elsa. *Muhammad of Mecca: Prophet of Islam*. New York: Franklin Watts, 2001.

McFarlane, Marilyn. *Sacred Myths: Stories of World Religions*. Portland, Oreg.: Sibyl Publications, 1996.

Morris, Neil. *Islam*. Columbus, Ohio: Peter Bedrick Books, 2002.

Penney, Sue. *Islam*. Chicago, Heinemann Library, 2000.

Wood, Angela. *Muslim Mosque*. Milwaukee, Wisc.: Gareth Stevens Publishing, 2000.

Internet Sites

IslamiCity.com
(Comprehensive multimedia website featuring news concerning the world of Islam; Muslim beliefs, history, and culture; audio recitations of the Qur'an; radio and cyberTV links; online shopping; recipes; and a virtual hajj)
http://www.islam.org

IslamOnline.net
(Online resource devoted to all things Islamic; includes current affairs, details on *Ramadan* and other observances, hajj, and the full text of three translations of the Qur'an)
http://www.islam-online.net

PBS: Islam, Empire of Faith
(Companion website to the PBS film; includes four timelines based on faith, culture, innovation, and people; video clips; and lessons on the basic principles of Islam)
http://www.pbs.org/empires/islam

Index